Night
Classical
Volume 1

Night

Poetry from the
Classical Persian Canon
Volume 1

Selected and adapted by
Abbas Kiarostami

A translation by
Iman Tavassoly and Paul Cronin

Sticking Place Books
New York

Shiva Sheybany
Sohrab Mahdavi
Stacey Knecht
and
Michael Beard
are thanked by the translators

© Sticking Place Books 2016
www.stickingplacebooks.com
www.lessonswithkiarostami.com

Design by Ryan Bojanovic

All rights reserved.
No part of this book may be reproduced, stored in or introduced into a retrieval system, or transmitted, in any form or by any means (electronic, mechanical, photocopying, recording or otherwise) without the written permission of the publishers, except in the case of brief quotations in critical articles or reviews.

ISBN 978-1-942782-20-9

Between 2006 and 2011, Iranian film director Abbas Kiarostami – author of three books of original verse – released his selections from and adaptations of four masters of Persian poetry: Nima (1895–1960), Hafez, Saadi and Rumi (all from the thirteenth and fourteenth centuries). This material is presented to English-speaking readers for the first time, in eight volumes: Hafez's *Wine*, Saadi's *Tears*, Nima's *Water* and Rumi's *Fire*. In 2015, Kiarostami published two further books, the thematic anthology *Night*, his selections from a variety of classical and contemporary poets, the English translation of which is issued in four volumes.

Kiarostami's project has been a contentious one, and in plucking fragments of poetry from longer works – an endeavour no less personal than the composition of original verse – he incurred the ire of critics in Iran. Some, whose lifelong pursuit has been the examination of the poets whose work Kiarostami presents in his volumes, believe him to be something of a dilettante, an interloper who lacks the skills required to handle this precious material. With no professional training in Persian literature, he is, they submit, unprepared for the task at hand, and some refuse to consider his work as legitimate poetry. In Iran, after all, poetry is treated with absolute seriousness, its authors regarded as the unveilers of vital secrets, endowed with powerful sensibilities, in effect keepers and revealers of the Persian soul. Certain books of verse are even treated as if they were holy texts, and it would not be unfair to suggest that the work of a handful of pivotal poets has profoundly influenced both the Persian language and, in turn, the daily lives of millions in modern Iran.

Still, along with criticism came praise. In publishing his straightforward selections for the general reader, it was noted that Kiarostami – whose work in any discipline attracts global attention – has opened up the world of Persian poetry to those largely unaware of this wondrous and vast body of work, especially readers beyond the borders of his homeland. "Some people, sitting at a dining table covered in fabulous food, don't know which dish to start with," says the meditative Kiarostami. These books are his way of navigating readers through that particular feast. Absorb and begin to understand these adaptations – "trailers," Kiarostami calls them – and we are, he believes, better equipped to tackle the originals in their fuller forms. There are many costly, ornate and ostentatious editions of poetry in Iran. But, says Kiarostami, such illuminated books exist "to be given as gifts, and rarely do they actually encourage reading." The opposite could be said of Kiarostami's versions: relatively inexpensive and unembellished, containing nothing but text. His self-professed and modest aim is to make an unequivocal and intimate connection between poem and reader, author and explorer.

So what precisely has Kiarostami done with the original texts? For his two *Night* volumes, he located lines of verse from an assortment of poets – venerable and present-day – each somehow relating to a single subject matter, and brought them together. ("It's worth noting," says Kiarostami, "that few of the poets write about what night actually is. Instead, the darkness and approaching dawn are used as reflections of feelings and inner conditions.") With all others, he has trimmed down poems by individual authors, pulled lines out of context and framed them piece by piece, at the same time retaining and thereby emphasising what he considers to be key concepts, characters and landscapes. Kiarostami has suggested that the unexpurgated originals are like crude oil, straight from the ground, in need of processing and refinement. By making his selections, deconstructing and breaking the metre of the original verse, cracking it open and removing the rhythm, Kiarostami has allowed specific ideas and themes to flow out in epigrammatic form. His reductionist method might be best understood by comparing a feature film, with its sweeping lines of narrative and interlocking characters, to a series of still photographs, each of which presents a single scene within a carefully constructed frame. It is as if Kiarostami has stood before a vast image, studied it carefully, isolated the elements he wants to accentuate, then affixed a frame over just one small part, so bringing to light something previously indistinct, almost unnoticeable, hitherto concealed.

Kiarostami's own poems are, more than anything, closest to Japanese Haiku, which is for the most part the form he has imposed upon his selections from the great masters. But in furnishing us with a mere three or four lines, Kiarostami – a practitioner of free verse, in both his adapted and original poetry – has striven to convey the essence, the fundamental meaning, of entire pages in the original. The result is a summary: poetry of minimalism. There is a startling compactness and simplicity to these books, with nothing extraneous, even if each page contains a discrete message and definite wisdom.

Kiarostami's process of creative condensation is uncomplicated and, to a large extent, intuitive. "In Paris one day I saw a book through a shop window," he explains. "On the cover was an enlargement of the corner of a Cezanne painting. It showed only an apple. The designer of the book cover hadn't negated the rest of the painting so much as magnified a piece of it, and by doing so asked the reader to explore this one piece of fruit. A poem is like wine, which should be enjoyed line by line, drop by drop. If you want to express love or hatred, or have been asked a question by someone, these books provide you with a great many potential responses. Younger readers will presumably appreciate their brevity, that they could be sent as graceful text messages. What's important is what the poet writes about. This is my priority, rather than how he tells it. I think more about effect than form. My duty is to transfer ideas to the audience. If this is best done in short bursts, if we are living in an age of concision, then so be it. It's important for me always to be experimenting, to re-think the kind of storytelling I involve myself with." Kiarostami explains little, instead pointing at what we should be looking at, proposing that we decipher things for ourselves. Almost every poem, however short, has more than one level of meaning and is therefore open to interpretation, although Kiarostami has suggested that the first message the reader arrives at is likely the one the poet, and Kiarostami himself, intended.

This is a body of work which for Kiarostami, who for decades had no intention of publishing his selections, has been a long time coming. "When I took Rumi's book in hand," he explains, "I realised that I had already done much of the required work because for twenty years I have been obsessively highlighting and isolating certain poems." At a Tehran event marking the publication of his Rumi volumes, Kiarostami offered a forthright explanation for his poetry project. "I hope you forgive my foolish courage. My aim with these books was never to integrate myself into the world of literature. This endeavour which I have undertaken – these selections, many of which are lesser-known verses – is not me meddling in your own work. I was consumed by literature and poetry long before I became a filmmaker." Whether or not the following are poems or aphorisms in disguise, this book – and every one of his published volumes of verse – represent deeply felt enthusiasms. As such, consider them an essential component of Kiarostami's oeuvre, one that includes films, photographs and installations. Put any number of his poems alongside, for example, *The Wind Will Carry Us*, or his still images of snowy landscapes, or "Forest Without Leaves," his three-dimensional art project consisting of hollow tubes, standing floor to ceiling, covered by life-size photographs of bark, and they take on an ever greater significance. The associations between all four forms of expression, the similarities in visual motifs and concepts, the common elements, the unity between settings, characters and themes all become quickly apparent. Whether using a camera, paintbrush, pen or (at home, quietly away from public view) wood chisel, Kiarostami's innermost preoccupations reveal themselves. Whichever vehicle he uses, again and again the same images and ideas are transported into the mind of the audience.

Chapter divisions in Kiarostami's Hafez book are his own, based on the subjects of the poems. Classical Persian poetry is traditionally arranged in reference to the final letter of each line. Kiarostami's original Saadi book is presented, chapter by chapter, in this way, but our translation is not (we have discarded all chapter divisions, while keeping the poems in exactly the same order). Kiarostami himself dropped from his Rumi book the traditional arrangement based on each line's final letter. In all of Kiarostami's adaptations, his alignment of poetry on the page is very much his own (including the layout, with one poem per page). While Hafez writes in the symmetrical ghazal form, Kiarostami breaks down this structure based on his own preferences. Likewise, where Kiarostami might use three lines, we use only two. The original Persian editions of these poems contain a number of errors, so in bringing these volumes to press we aim to present the most accurate versions of Kiarostami's adapted poetry available. There is occasional overlap between Kiarostami's single-author books and *Night*, with a small number of poems appearing in both.

As neither poets nor professional translators, we offer these fairly literal translations – something of a massive addendum to *Lessons with Kiarostami*, a book detailing Kiarostami's recognisably poetic approach to filmmaking, published simultaneously – at the very least so they may unveil some of the mainsprings of his work as a storyteller and creator of images, thereby offering insight into his work as a filmmaker.

Iman Tavassoly and Paul Cronin

Dark night.
Fear of waves.
Fearsome whirlpool.
How can they
who rest upon the seashore
understand us?

شب تاریک و
بیم موج و گردابی چنین هایل
کجا دانند حال ما
سبکباران ساحل ها

Hafez

Conversations with kings are darkness on the longest night.

Seek light from the sun, which hopefully will rise.

حافظ

صحبتِ حکّام
ظلمتِ شبِ یلداست

نور ز خورشید جوی بو که برآید

Helali Jagata'i

No night was as dark as this night.

Tonight it seems there was neither light nor moon.

هلالی جغتایی

هیچ شب
این چنین سیاه نبود

گویی امشب چراغ ماه نبود

Attar

Ignorant as you are,
night and day,
of day and night,
how do you expect
day and night's secret
to bring you joy?

عطّار

روز و شب چون غافلی از روز و شب
کی کنی از سرِّ روز و شب طرب

Saib Tabrizi

The mystery is one of respecting love's rituals.
At night, birds leave the flying to butterflies.

صائب تبریزی

رمزی است ز پاس ادب عشق،
که مرغان
شب نوبت پرواز
به پروانه گذارند

Day is for business and trade.

Desire for night is something else.

Rumi

روز اگر مکسب و سوداگری است

ذوق دگر دارد سودای شب

مولوی

Her lips, words, hair and face

are wine and sugar and night and moonlight.

Khwaju Kermani

لب و گفتار و زلف و عارضِ اوست

باده و شکّر و شب و مهتاب

خواجوی کرمانی

Jami

Half your life is day.
The other is night with shining stars.

جامی

هست یکی نیمهٔ عمرِ تو روز
نیمهٔ دیگر
شبِ انجم فروز

Iqbal

She allowed no one's night to darken.
In every heart does light burn with longing for her.

اقبال

شبِ کس در جهان تاریک نگذاشت
که در هر دل ز داغ او چراغ است

Iraqi

This is the night of separation.
What will tomorrow bring?

I long for the morning of my hope to be filled with light.

عراقی

شبِ هجر است، تا فردا چه زاید

مگر روشن شود صبح امیدم

Farrukhi Sistani

"You do not know what this dark night
will give birth to,"
I said.
Be patient.
Let it deliver.

فرخی سیستانی

گفتم تو چه دانی
که شبِ تیره چه زاید
بشکیب و صبوری کن
تا شب بنهد بار

Abusa'id Abolkhayr

Each day until night
do I live with one thousand sorrows.

I will see what divine judgment unveils behind the curtain.

ابوسعید ابوالخیر

روزی به هزار غم
به شب می آرم

تا خود فلک از پرده چه آرد بیرون

Vahshi Bafqi

I longed for a day of joy
to be delivered from fate.
I had no idea that
fate is pregnant
with the longest night of the year,
which brings with it for me
one thousand sorrows.

وحشی بافقی

روز عیشی خواستم زایَد
چه دانستم که چرخ
حامله دارد به صد ماتم
شبِ یلدای من

Hafez

Dark night.
Fear of waves.
Fearsome whirlpool.

How can those who rest upon the seashore understand us?

حافظ

شب تاریک و بیم موج و
گردابی چنین هایل

کجا دانند حال ما سبکباران ساحل ها

Salman Savoji

Night.
Desert.
Wind.
I am lost.

Only a hidden fortune can guide me.

سلمان ساوجی

شب است و بادیه و باد و من چنین گمره
مگر سعادتی از غیب، رهنمون آید

Iraqi

Bound to the hair of the beloved.
We expect some resolution to this dark night.

عراقی

در سرِ زلفِ یار
دل بندیم
که به روز آید آخرِ این
شبِ تار

Khaqani

There is for me every week
one night of solitude
for which I would not trade
the other six days.

خاقانی

این یک شبِ خلوت
که به هرِ هفته مرا هست
حقا که به شش روزِ مسلم
نفروشم

Ferdowsi

Night dark as tar.
Hidden moon.

Birds and animals sleeping.

فردوسی

شبی قیرگون
ماه پنهان شده

به خواب اندرون مرغ و دام و دده

Hafez

Dark night.
Desert.
I will get nowhere

unless the candle of your face shines upon the path.

حافظ

شبِ ظلمت و بیابان
به کجا توان رسیدن

مگر آن که شمع رویت به رهم چراغ دارد

Vahshi Bafqi

You are unaware of the story of night.

No ear is as deaf as yours.

وحشی بافقی

از قصهٔ شب
تو را خبر نیست

چون گوش تو هیچ گوش کر نیست

Khwaju Kermani

Not a night passes
without pleading to the sky.

But what can I do? There is no saviour.

خواجوی کرمانی

شب نیست،
که فریاد به گردون نرسانم

لیکن چه توان کرد که فریادرسی نیست

Attar

Day and night
rush and roar
as they travel through
narrow curtains
of the mind.

عطّار

در جوش و در خروش از آنند روز و شب
کز تنگنای پردهٔ پندار می روند

Rumi

For us
there is no difference
between night and day.

No difference if the sun rises or sets.

مولوی

چه باشد شب
چه باشد روز ما را

که خورشید ار فرو شُد، ار برآمد

Saadi

Ask those awake how long is the night.

It seems short to those sleeping.

سعدی

درازنای شب از
ناخفتگان پرس

که خواب آلوده را کوته نماید

Helali Jagata'i

Wakefulness,
nights
and me.
Calling on God
from night until morning.

God! Let no one see such nights even when dreaming.

هلالی جغتایی

من و بیداری و شب‌ها
و شب تا روز یا رب‌ها

نبیند هیچ کس در خواب یا رب این چنین شب‌ها

For others, days of joy and happiness.

For me, dark nights and tears.

Fayz Kashani

غیر را روزهای عیش و طرب

من و
شب های تار و زاری ها

فیض کاشانی

Iraqi

Our soul howls through the day.

A heart filled with pain. Tears from night until morning.

عراقی

نعره ز جان زنیم
همه روز تا به شب

ناله ز درد دل، همه شب تا سحر کنیم

Helali Jagata'i

As dark night arrived
tears were shed
by the heart of the dervish.

هلالی جغتایی

چون شبِ تیره در میان آمد
دل درویش در فغان آمد

Rumi

Those asleep are unaware of night.

Angels host divine guests.

مولوی

از شب چه خبر باشد مر مردم خوابی را

هم کاسه ملک باشد مهمان خدایی را

The moon is cold, wet, colourful.

It walks through night.
Restless.
Wandering.

Anvari

ماه سرد و ترست و رنگ آمیز

شب دو و بی قرار و هر جایی

انوری

Saadi

Every night
I have another thought
and a different conclusion.

Should I depart tomorrow because of you?

سعدی

هر شب
اندیشهٔ دیگر کنم و رای دگر

که من از دستِ تو فردا بروم جای دگر

Fayz Kashani

Endless night and day saddened me.

How joyful is that place free of day and night.

فیض کاشانی

زین شب و روز مکرر دل گرفت

ای خوش آن جایی که صبح و شام نیست

Anvari

Wherever is your hair is night.

Wherever is your face is sunshine.

انوری

آن جا که زلفِ توست همه یکسره شب است

وآنجا که روی توست همه یکسرِ آفتاب

No wonder your dark hair sits on either side of your face.

Each day between two nights.

Helali Jagata'i

روی تو در آن دو زلف مشکین، چه عجب

هر روز که هست
در میان دو شب است

هلالی جغتایی

Saadi

The candle and I burn at night.

My flames inside.

سعدی

شب ها
من و شمع می گدازیم

این است که سوز من نهان است

Hafez

Nightwatchman
of heart's sanctuary am I.
Night after night

I think only about her behind this curtain.

حافظ

پاسبانِ حرمِ دل شده ام شب همه شب

تا در این پرده جز اندیشهٔ او نگذارم

Vahshi Bafqi

Tonight is my feverish sorrow
more intense
than other nights.

Look after me this night.

وحشی بافقی

ز شب‌های دگر دارم
تب غم بیشترِ امشب

وصیت می‌کنم باشید از من باخبرِ امشب

O heart!
Stay away from her dimple, concealed behind beautiful hair.

This night is dark.
Watch out for a water well upon the path.

Foroughi Bastami

ای دل از زلفِ دلاویزش مکن قصدِ زنخدان

شب بسی تار است
بنگر در رهت چاهی نباشد

فـروغی بسطامی

Hatef Esfehani

"I will shed your blood some other night,"
she told me yesterday.
I hope tonight she remembers those words.

هاتف اصفهانی

دوش می‌گفت
که خونت شبِ دیگر ریزم
امشب امید که یاد از سخنِ دوشش باد

Fayz Kashani

I sit at night
in remembrance of your eyebrows.
I turn my back on sleep.
I turn my face to sanctuary.

فیض کاشانی

شب نشستم، به یاد ابرویت
پشت بر خواب و
روی در محراب

Saadi

The night of impatient lovers is a long night.

Come! From the start of night is the door of morning open.

سعدی

شب عاشقان بی دل
چه شبی دراز باشد

تو بیا که از اول شب، در صبح باز باشد

Hafez

Dark night of separation.
Me, near death.

Time for you to rise like a shining moon.

حافظ

در تیرهٔ شبِ هجرِ توأم
جان به لب آمد

وقت است که همچون مَهِ تابان به در آیی

Helali Jagata'i

Every night, without you.
Me and my corner of solitude.

My feet buried in sorrow. My heavy head.

هلالی جغتایی

بی تو هرِ شب منم و
گوشهٔ تنهایی خویش

پای در دامنِ غم، سر به گریبان ملال

Iraqi

Impossible this dark night
to hide on your estate.
Such light from your face!

عراقی

ز روشنایی روی تو در شبِ تاریک
نمی‌توان به سرِ کوی تو، نهان آمد

No wonder my heart was blind to daylight.

Your hair encloses
the one hundred longest nights
of the year.

Fayz Kashani

چه عجب گر دل من روز ندید

زلفِ تو صد شبِ یلدا دارد

فیض کاشانی

Union with the beloved is like a sun that for me never rises.

This dark night of separation for me has no end.

Fayz Kashani

آفتابِ وصلِ جانان بر نمی آید مرا

وین شبِ تاریکِ هجران سر نمی آید مرا

فیض کاشانی

Khaqani

Separation.
Every night I weep to God.

God weeps because of my tears.

خاقانی

هر شب ز دست هجرش چندان به یارب آیم

کز دست یارب من یارب به یارب آید

Last night there was no hope for morning,
so pained by your love was I.

The prisoner of love cannot tolerate long nights.

Saadi

ز درد عشق تو دوشم امید صبح نبود

اسیرِ عشق
چه تابِ شبِ دراز آرد

سعدی

Orfi Shirazi

Let my night be long.
Dawn is there.
I am here.

عرفی شیرازی

دراز باد شبم
با سحر چه کار مرا

Ubayd Zakani

The pain of the heart
tells a story.
Sorrow of long nights.

Not a story that can readily see light of day.

عبید زاکانی

قصهٔ درد دل و
غصهٔ شب‌های دراز

صورتی نیست که جایی بتوان گفتن باز

Hafez

Leave out the story of the night of separation

and so appreciate her unveiling on the day of union.

حافظ

حکایت شبِ هجران
فروگذاشته به

به شُکرِ آن که برافکند پرده روزِ وصال

Foroughi Bastami

O Foroughi!
On this night of separation
let there be patience until dawn.

فروغی بسطامی

کاش فروغی
شبِ هجرانِ دوست
تا به سحر، تاب و توانت دهند

Fayz Kashani

Being with you
turns everyone else's night into day.
Sorrow of separation turns my day to night.

فیض کاشانی

شبِ اغیار ز دیدارِ تو روز
روزِ من از غمِ هجرانِ تو شب

Khaqani

All night
just me
and a light.

My companion until daytime.

خاقانی

تنها همه شب من و چراغی

مونس شده تا به گاه روزم

I resolved to be close to your face and hair
from morning until night.

Eventual separation turned my day into dark night.

Salman Savoji

با رخ و زلف تو گفتم که به روز آرم شب

عاقبت هجرِ تو،
روزم به شب تارَ آورد

سلمان ساوجی

Helali Jagata'i

Life is gone.
Dark night of separation did not end.

Either my night should have been shorter or my life longer.

هلالی جغتایی

عمرِ بگذشت و
شبِ تاریکِ هجر آخر نشد

یا شبم کوتاه می بایست، یا عمرم دراز

Fayz Kashani

Night of separation.
Sorrow upon sorrow.

Day of union with you. Happiness and joy.

فیض کاشانی

شب هجرانِ تو
غم بر سرِ غم

روز وصلت همه شادی و طرب

Saadi

Night.
I go to bed with the sorrow of separation

if that day I have not embraced you.

سعدی

هر شبم با غمِ هجرانِ تو سر بر بالین

روزی ار با تو نشد دست در آغوش مرا

Foroughi Bastami

Glimpse her beauty
and you will understand
why day and night of separation
are so dark.

فروغی بسطامی

روشنت گردد اگر خال و خطش را بینی
که چرا روزِ فراق و شبِ هجران تار است

My morning of union cannot transcend
the mountain of separation.

The day of my hope is dark as night.

Iraqi

صبح وصال بماند در پس کوه فراق

روز امیدم چو شب
تیره و ظلمانی است

عراقی

Vahshi Bafqi

Too long is the night of separation.
Especially tonight.

I long for day after this night of separation.

وحشی بافقی

شب هجران چه دراز است
خصوصاً این شب

کاش روزی ز پس این شب هجران بودی

Khaqani

Ask the night of separation how I am.

See how I burn in flames of desire.

خاقانی

از شبِ هجران بپرس تا به چه روزم

ز آتش سودا ببین، که در چه گدازم

Roudaki

Every night I think:
God!
If this is separation,
what would union be like?

رودکی

اندیشه کنم
هرِ شب و گویم: یا رب
هجرانش چنین است،
وصالش چون است؟

Fayz Kashani

If the entire surface of the earth were a notebook,
the story of the night of separation would not fit.

فیض کاشانی

به فرضِ اگر،
همه روی زمین شود دفتر
حکایتِ شبِ هجران
در او نمی گنجد

Saadi

Who can tell the story of the night of separation?

Only whoever counts stars like Saadi.

سعدی

حکایت شب هجران
که باز داند گفت

مگر کسی که چو سعدی ستاره بشمارد

Helali Jagata'i

Alas!
Life consumed by nights of separation.
I still do not know what the day of union is.

هلالی جغتایی

دردا که عمرِ در شبِ هجرانِ گذشت
و من
آگه نیم هنوز که روز وصال چیست؟

Impossible for the world to be filled with light in your absence.

Sun and night cannot come together.

Anvari

کی دهد کار جهان نور و تو غایب ز جهان

شب و خورشید به هم
هر دو کجا آید راست

انوری

Khwaju Kermani

If every morning you cannot hear me weeping,
who then will rescue me from nights of separation?

خواجوی کرمانی

گر به گوشَت نرسد صبحدمی فریادم
که رسد در شبِ هجرانِ تو فریاد مرا

Salman Savoji

The night of separation has an unforgettable effect.

It is the morning of union of which one can find no trace.

سلمان ساوجی

شبِ هجرانِ تو را هست، به غایت اثری

صبحِ وصل است که هیچش اثری پیدا نیست

Abusa'id Abolkhayr

You are aware of my suffering this night of separation.

Are you aware of my daytime suffering?

ابوسعید ابوالخیر

داری خبر از سوزِ شبِ هجرانم

آیا چه خبر ز سوز روزم داری

The heart, afraid of separation.

It seems that the day of union
is the same as the night of separation.

Anvari

چنان ترسد دل از هجرِ تو گویی

شبِ هجرانِ تو، روز وصال است

انوری

Saadi

The night of separation
is the longest night of the year.

God! Free them all, those in captivity.

سعدی

شب فراق تو
هر شب که هست یلدایی است

خلاص بخش خدایا، همه اسیران را

Gha'ani

As you reveal your face
from behind your hair
the sun rises
on the longest night of the year.

قاآنی

چون از خم زلف
چهره بنمایی
خورشید برآید از
شبِ یلدا

Iraqi

I do not mean to complain,
but you, so kind,
should you not be doing something to help?
"Every night a tired man sheds tears upon my door."

عراقی

گیرم که من نگویم
لطف تو خود نگوید،
کاین خسته چند نالد هر شب
بر آستانم!

Khaqani

Many nights did I spend longing for you.

Why withhold your dawn breeze from me?

خاقانی

به امید تو
بسا شب، که به روز کردم از غم

تو چرا نسیمت از من به سحر دریغ داری؟

Saib Tabrizi

Do not turn your face from us.
Our midnight sighs
have turned many bright mornings
into night.

صائب تبریزی

از ما متاب روی
که از آه نیم شب
بسیار صبح آینه را
شام کرده ایم

Sanai

My life without you is dark, no?
Nights of longing for union are restless, yes?

سنایی

یا سیاه و تیره بی تو روزگارم
نیست، هست
یا بر امیدِ وصالت
شب قرارم هست، نیست

Rumi

Ever since that night
when you revealed your moon to lovers,
everyone has been restless,
just as the world is restless.

مولوی

زان شب که ماه خویش
نمودی به عاشقان
چون چرخِ بی قرار
کسی را قرَار نیست

Attar

If every night
you burn like a candle,
at dawn
will you be rewarded.

عطّار

گر بسوزی تا سحر
هر شب چو شمع
تحفه از نقدِ سحرگاهت دهند

Rumi

The heart that tonight longs for union with you
will tomorrow surely be blessed.

مولوی

هر دل که با هوای تو
امشب شود حریف
او را یقین بدان تو که فردا مبارک است

Vahshi Bafqi

Thinking at night
about sorrow of day
destroys me.

Daytime thinking about nighttime suffering destroys me.

وحشی بافقی

شب هلاکم می کند
اندیشهٔ غم های روز

روز فکرِ محنت شب های تارم می کشد

Attar

Every day
I burnt in your love
from morning until night.
Burn me
like a miserable candle
every night
until dawn.

عطّار

هر روز تا به شب
چو ز عشق تو سوختم
هر شب، چو شمع زار
مرا تا سحر بسوز

Saib Tabrizi

The tears of the candle
are not for the butterfly.
Dawn closes in.
The candle worries
about its own dark night.

صائب تبریزی

گریهٔ شمع
از برای ماتم پروانه نیست
صبح نزدیک است،
در فکرِ شبِ تارِ خود است

Abusa'id Abolkhayr

What else can the lover do
but be humble?
What else can he do
but come every night to your door?

ابوسعید ابوالخیر

عاشق که تواضع ننماید
چه کند
شب‌ها که به کوی تو نیاید
چه کند

Rumi

Day.
Night.
I know neither.

What is there to know? Who is there to know?
O beloved! You count the days.

مولوی

خواه شب و خواه سحر
نیستم از هر دو، خبر

کیست خبر چیست خبر روزشماری صنما

Shah Nematollah Vali

We are love itself.
Our heart is restless night and day.

شاه نعمت الله ولی

عین عشقیم
لاجرم شب و روز
صبر و آرام در دلِ ما نیست

Attar

Every night
comes affliction
from the cruelty of life.

Every moment of life spent in pain.

عطّار

هر شب ز جور چرخ بلایی دگر رسید

هر دم ز روز عمر به دردی دگر گذشت

Rumi

We enter into turmoil of night,
and make waves in night's ocean.

مولوی

چونک در آییم به غوغای شب
گرد برآریم ز دریای شب

Salman Savoji

At night,
desirous of her,
I make happy my heart
by hoping for tomorrow.
But I am afraid that this night of longing
may have no tomorrow.

سلمان ساوجی

من در شبِ سودای او،
دل خوش به فردا می‌کنم
لیکن شبِ سودای او
ترسم که بی فردا بُود

Shah Nematollah Vali

Divine night.
If you were men of wisdom,
you would see moon and sun both.

شاه نعمت الله ولی

گر چه شبِ قدر است
چو صاحب نظرانید
چون روز در این شب
مه و خورشید ببینید

I cannot live a day without you.

I cannot sleep a night without you.

Sanai

بی تو یک روز بود، نتوانم

بی تو یک شب غنود، نتوانم

سنایی

Rumi

On the night of union, my night turns to day.

I swear to God, how good it will be!
No more counting days and nights.

مولوی

شبِ وصال بیاید
شبم چو روز شود

که روز و شب نشمارم چه خوش بود به خدا

Saadi! Tell the story of the sorrow she brought forth

and night will end before your story does.

Saadi

سعدیا گر همه شب شرحِ غمش خواهی گفت

شب به پایان رود و
شرح به پایان نرود

سعدی

All night have I wept too much because of life.

Every night two hundred of my tears touch the sky.

Helali Jagata'i

بس که در ناله ام از گردش گردون همه شب

هیچ شب نیست
دو صد ناله به گردون نشود

هلالی جغتایی

Iraqi

My nightly cries and sighs
are those of joy
when standing on your doorstep.

عراقی

ناله و فریادِ من هر نیم شب
بر درِ وصلت
تقاضایی خوش است

Hafez

Ask the morning breeze.
It knows that the scent of your hair
is our soul's companion
from night until dawn.

حافظ

از صبا پرس که ما را همه شب
تا دم صبح، بوی زلف تو
همان مونسِ جان است که بود

Because of her, my night of joy was filled with daylight.

Alas! Alas!
She departed and my day became dark as night.

Helali Jagata'i

آن که چون روز، شب عیشم ازاو روشن بود

رفت و روزم چو شب تار شد، افسوس، افسوس

هلالی جغتایی

Fayz Kashani

Your hair dark as night.
The shining sun hides,
waiting to rise
on the day of reckoning.

فیض کاشانی

در شامِ زلفت، خورشیدِ تابان
پنهان در آن شب، روزِ قیامت

Rumi

Day.
I see you.
Night.
Sorrow of separation.

O beloved! You turn night to day.

مولوی

روز مرا دیدن تو
شب غم ببریدن تو

از تو شبم روز شود همچو نهاری صنما

Saadi

In my mind,
nights without you
are dark as the grave.
Should dawn arrive without you,
it will be the day of reckoning.

سعدی

شب‌های بی توام
شب گور است در خیال
ور بی تو بامداد کنم، روز محشر است

Hafez

Your beauty makes the world beautiful.
Without it, my day is like night.

In your absence my tears burn the world like a candle.

حافظ

بی جمال عالَم آرای تو
روزم چون شب است

ورنه از آهی جهانی را بسوزانم چو شمع

Helali Jagata'i

Darkness of night descended.
The dervish, tormented by separation.

هلالی جغتایی

باز چون ظلمتِ شب آمد پیش
مبتلای فراق شد درویش

Helali Jagata'i

Whoever separated me from you
and so turned day into night,
may his day be as dark as my life.

هلالی جغتایی

آن که روزم را سیه کرد از فراقت همچو شب
روزِ او چون روزگارِ من سیه باد از فراق

Vahshi Bafqi

Good fortune upon you.
Sleep joyously.
If you need a guard,
at midnight I will pray
and fill the world
with an army.

وحشی بافقی

تو خوش به دولت خواب کن
گر پاسبانی بایدت
من از دعای نیم شب
گردون پر از لشکر کنم

Salman Savoji

"Morning breeze will bring you news from me,"
you said.
Tell this to someone
who expects morning to follow night.

سلمان ساوجی

گفته ای:
باد صبا با تو بگوید، خبرم
این خبر پیشِ کسی گو،
که شبش را سحری است

Helali Jagata'i

To spend night until morning with you
I would need a night longer than the day of reckoning.

هلالی جغتایی

از بهرِ آن که با تو
شبی آورم به روز
خواهم شبی
ز روزِ قیامت درازتر

The night you become nothing brings forth light.
Progress upon the path to mysticism.

Seek the value of a candle
on the longest night of the year.

Vahshi Bafqi

رتبهٔ عرفان شود، شام فنا روشن است

قیمت انوار شمع
در شبِ یلدا طلب

وحشی بافقی

Hafez

Hafez!
Turn your back on every myth.
Drink wine for a moment.
Last night we did not sleep.
The candle burnt like a myth.

حافظ

ترک افسانه بگو حافظ و می نوش دمی
که نخفتیم شب و شمع به افسانه بسوخت

Sanai

You ask why all night I never sleep.
The eyes of lovers must never sleep.

سنایی

مرا گویی که بیداری همه شب
دو چشمِ عاشقان بیدار باید

Saadi

No rest for me this night of separation.
No patience from me this day of union.

سعدی

شب هجرانم آرمیدن نیست
روز وصلم قرارِ دیدن نیست

Hafez

Bring no candle to this gathering.
At our nighttime festivities
the face of the beloved
shines as does the moon,
a full moon.

حافظ

گو شمع میارید در این جمع
که امشب
در مجلس ما ماهِ رخ دوست
تمام است

Rumi

A night spent with restless heart,
longing for you,
shall by day shine brightly upon the world.

مولوی

هر دل که او نخفت شبی در هوای تو
چون روز روشن است و هوا زو منور است

Saadi

No one asks you how long is the night.

Whoever knows is last night's sleepless one.

سعدی

از تو نپرسند درازای شب

آن کس داند، که نخفته است دوش

Rumi

Your face, a full moon.
Tonight, divine night.

O queen of beauties! Sleep not tonight.

مولوی

روی تو چو بَدر آمد
امشب شبِ قدر آمد

ای شاهِ همه خوبان، زنهار مخسب امشب

He turned his back on every impurity.

He neither slept at night
nor rested during the day.

Jami

شُست از آلودگی، به کلی دست

نه به شب خفت و
نی به روز نشست

جامی

Attar

He neither slept at night
nor rested during the day,

so reached the point of self-sacrifice.

عطّار

شب نخفت و به روز نارامید

تا ز هستی خود به جان آمد

Saadi

All night we fail to sleep.

O you who have been sleeping your entire life! Beware!

سعدی

ما را همه شب نمی برد خواب

ای خفته روزگار دریاب

Foroughi Bastami

I was unaware of the day of reckoning.
The night of separation
was created as the longest night of the year.

فروغی بسطامی

من از روزِ جزا واقف نبودم
شبِ یلدای هجران آفریدند

We did not appreciate the day of union.

On the night of separation
our worries kept us awake.

Saadi

جز ای آن که نگفتیم شکر روز وصال

شب فراق نخفتیم لاجرم
ز خیال

سعدی

Foroughi Bastami

Whoever is not awake to your love
through the night
will never deserve good fortune.

فروغی بسطامی

در خورِ دولت، بیدار نگردد هرگز
آن که شب تا سحر، از عشقِ تو بیدار نماند

Mohtasham Kashani

Thinking about you
keeps me sleepless
every night.

I want sleep, but worries frustrate it.

محتشم کاشانی

مرا خیال تو
شب‌ها به خواب نگذارد

چو تن به خواب دهم، اضطراب نگذارد

Saadi

Day of separation.
"Good night," I said to sleep.

سعدی

روز فراقِ دوستان
شب خوش بگفتم خواب را

Khwaju Kermani

For how long,
each night,
should the sanctuary candle and I burn?

For how long, each night, should we spend our lives
restless, wandering?

خواجوی کرمانی

چند سوزیم من و شمعِ شبستان همه شب

چند سازیم چنین بی سر و سامان همه شب

Nezami

Be mine,
for just one night,
amid one thousand nights.

نظامی

یک شب
ز هزار شب، مرا باش

Anvari

Me, awake all night until morning,

trailed by your sorrow.

انوری

همه شب تا به روز بیدارم

تا غمت می کشد گریبانم

Helali Jagata'i

On the night of separation
the heart is split into one thousand pieces.

Where are those joyful moments of union?

هلالی جغتایی

دارد هزار تفرقه دل در شبِ فراق

کو آن فراقتی که به روزِ وصال کرد؟

I died awaiting day of union with you.

Is there an end to this night of separation?

Iraqi

بمردم ز انتظارِ روزِ وصلت

شبِ هجران مگر پایان ندارد؟

عراقی

Fayz Kashani

Day and night,
remind the one beside the beloved:
"Think about the pains of those with hearts
burnt in separation."

فیض کاشانی

گو یاد کن
ز حالِ جگر خستگانِ هجر
آن را که هست روز و شب
اندر کنار دوست

Saadi

Night of separation.
Darkness,

even if one thousand moons arise.

سعدی

شبِ هجرانِ دوست
ظلمانی است

ور برآید هزار مهتابش

Alas! My life.

Nights.
Nights of separation.
Days.
Days of separation.

Hatef Esfehani

دردا و دریغا که بود عمرِ مرا

شبها شبِ هجر و
روزها روز فراق

هاتف اصفهانی

Hafez

Complaining about the night of separation
is no simple tale.

Describing one single glance requires one hundred books.

حافظ

شکایتِ شبِ هجران نه آن حکایتِ حال است

که شمّه‌ای ز بیانش، به صد رساله برآید

Vahshi Bafqi

Darkness of night.
We departed towards moonlight.

وحشی بافقی

از ظلمت شب
رخت به مهتاب کشیدیم

Ubayd Zakani

Moonlit night.
Springtime.

عبید زاکانی

شبِ مهتاب و
فصلِ نوبهاران

O heart! For how long will you beg for moonlight?

Inflame the night with your breath.

Iqbal

دلا دریوزهٔ مهتاب تا کی

شبِ خود را
برافروز از دمِ خویش

اقبال

Helali Jagata'i

Night of union.
Me, free of moonlight.

هلالی جغتایی

در شبِ وصل از
فروغِ ماهِ گردون فارغم

Hafez

Night of separation.
No shining stars.

Go to the roof of the palace and light up the moon.

حافظ

ستاره شبِ هجران
نمی‌فشاند نور

به بامِ قصر برآی و چراغِ مَه بَرکن

Fayz Kashani

Night of separation.
Creator of all darkness.
Day of union.
Bringer of morning.

فیض کاشانی

شبِ هجرِ تو جاعل الظلمات
روزِ وصلِ تو فالق الاصباح

Fayz Kashani

Contemplate dark night in the beloved's hair.

فیض کاشانی

در زلفِ یارِ
حالِ شبِ تار بنگرید

We wander through the beloved's hair.

Divine night.
Divine we become.

Rumi

چون در سرِ زلفِ یار پیچیم

اندر شبِ قدر
قدر، ما راست

مولوی

Attar

Not a day turns to night
when desire for your hair
does not send armies of affliction
from all four directions
into my heart.

عطّار

روز به شب نمی‌رسد
تا ز خیالِ زلفِ تو
بر دلِ من ز چارسو
خیلِ بلا نمی‌رسد

Attar

Night.
The world as dark as your hair.
No seeker.
No seeking.

عطّار

شبی که از زلف تو
عالم چو شب بود
سرِ مویی نه طالب
نه طلب بود

Salman Savoji

Reveal your face.
In the dark night of your hair
is my heart,
lost,
seeking moonlight.

سلمان ساوجی

بنمای رخ که در شبِ تاریکِ طره ات
دل گم شده است و راه
به مهتاب می برد

Ubayd Zakani

The story of the night of separation
and our predicament

is as long as the hair of beauties.

عبید زاکانی

شرحِ شبِ هجران و
پریشانی ما

چون زلف بتان دراز نایی دارد

Anvari

Every night a vision of your face comes to me,
turning my day to night as dark as your hair.

انوری

هر شب
خیالِ رویِ تو آید به پیشِ من
تا روزِ من کند به سیاهی چو موی تو

Saadi

No one knows how long is the night of separation,

save the one held captive in the prison of love.

سعدی

شبِ فراق که داند که تا سحر چند است

مگر کسی که به زندانِ عشق دربند است

Vahshi Bafqi

The night of separation visits us all,
bringing with it the longest night of the year.

وحشی بافقی

شامِ هجرانِ تو
تشریف به هر جا ببرد
در پس و پیش هزاران شبِ یلدا ببرد

On my knees, I declare union with you.

Is there an end to this night of separation?

Fayz Kashani

بگو بگو به وصالت که سخت سوگندی است

شبِ فراقِ تو را
هیچ انتهایی هست؟

فیض کاشانی

Salman Savoji

Night.
Desert.
The heart is lost.
Left.
Right.
Front.
Back.
There are water wells upon the path.

سلمان ساوجی

شب است و بادیه و دل، فتاده از راه است
ز چپ و راست، مخالف، ز پیش و پس، چاه است

Hafez

Dark night.
I have lost the path of desire.

O guiding star! Arise from anywhere!

حافظ

در این شبِ سیاهم
گم گشت راه مقصود

از گوشه ای برون آی ای کوکبِ هدایت

Helali Jagata'i

My day became night.
The moon did not pass by.

Such a futile life.
A year spent, but no moon passed by.

هلالی جغتایی

روزِ من شب شد و آن ماه به راهی نگذشت

این چه عمری است که سالی شد و ماهی نگذشت؟

Rumi

The road is long.
We run quickly across and alongside night.

مولوی

راه درازاست، برانیم تیز
ما به درازا و به پهنای شب

Hafez

Night is dark.
The path to safety lies before us.

Where is the fire of Sinai? When is our meeting?

حافظ

شبِ تار است و
ره وادی ایمن در پیش

آتش طور کجا موعدِ دیدار کجاست

Foroughi Bastami

Alas!
I walk upon the path of love,
alone,
joined only by nightly tears and morning sighs.

فروغی بسطامی

فریاد که جز اشکِ شب و
آهِ سحرگاه
اندر سفرِ عشق
مرا هم سفری نیست

Iraqi

The day of my fortune once again darkened
as does night.
The morning of my hope again darkened.

عراقی

روزِ بختِ من چو شبِ تاریک شد
صبحِ امیدم به شام افتاد باز

Rumi

Day and night
I am restless
in my desire for you.

Day and night my head upon your feet.

مولوی

در هوایت
بی‌قرارم روز و شب

سر ز پایت برندارم روز و شب

Fayz Kashani

Time for separation.
For how long do I await union?
Day of union never arrived.
Night of separation never departs.

فیض کاشانی

تا چند در فراقِ برم انتظارِ وصل
آن روز خود نیامد و
این شب نمی رود

Iqbal

Scatter my ashes at dawn.
Give me at least one night of joy.

اقبال

پریشان کن سحر خاکسترم را ولیکن
سوز و ساز یک شبم بخش

Attar

My day died.
Come to me at night.

I am the wanderer. Find a solution to my life.

عطّار

فرو شد روز من
یک شب برم آی

که تا کار من حیران برآید

Published by Sticking Place Books

Lessons with Kiarostami
Edited by Paul Cronin

A Wolf on Watch (dual-language)
Poems by Abbas Kiarostami

With the Wind (dual-language)
Poems by Abbas Kiarostami

Wind and Leaf (dual-language)
Poems by Abbas Kiarostami

Wine (dual-language)
Poetry by Hafez
Selected and adapted by Abbas Kiarostami

Tears (two volumes) (dual-language)
Poetry by Saadi
Selected and adapted by Abbas Kiarostami

Water (dual-language)
Poetry by Nima
Selected and adapted by Abbas Kiarostami

Fire (four volumes) (dual-language)
Poetry by Rumi
Selected and adapted by Abbas Kiarostami

Night (two volumes) (dual-language)
Poetry from the Classical Persian Canon
Selected and adapted by Abbas Kiarostami

Night (two volumes) (dual-language)
Poetry from the Contemporary Persian Canon
Selected and adapted by Abbas Kiarostami

In the Shadow of Trees
The Collected Poetry of Abbas Kiarostami

www.ingramcontent.com/pod-product-compliance
Lightning Source LLC
Chambersburg PA
CBHW042233090526
44588CB00005B/68